631ART.COM PRES[ENTS]

THE

BUDDAK·A·tS

IN

"INTERESTING FACTS ABOUT ANCIENT GREECE"

BY EDDIE ALFARO

ARCHIMEDES WAS AN ANCIENT GREEK MATHEMATICIAN, SCIENTIST AND INVENTOR. THE ARCHIMEDES' PRINCIPLE IS HIS MOST FAMOUS ACCOMPLISHMENT.

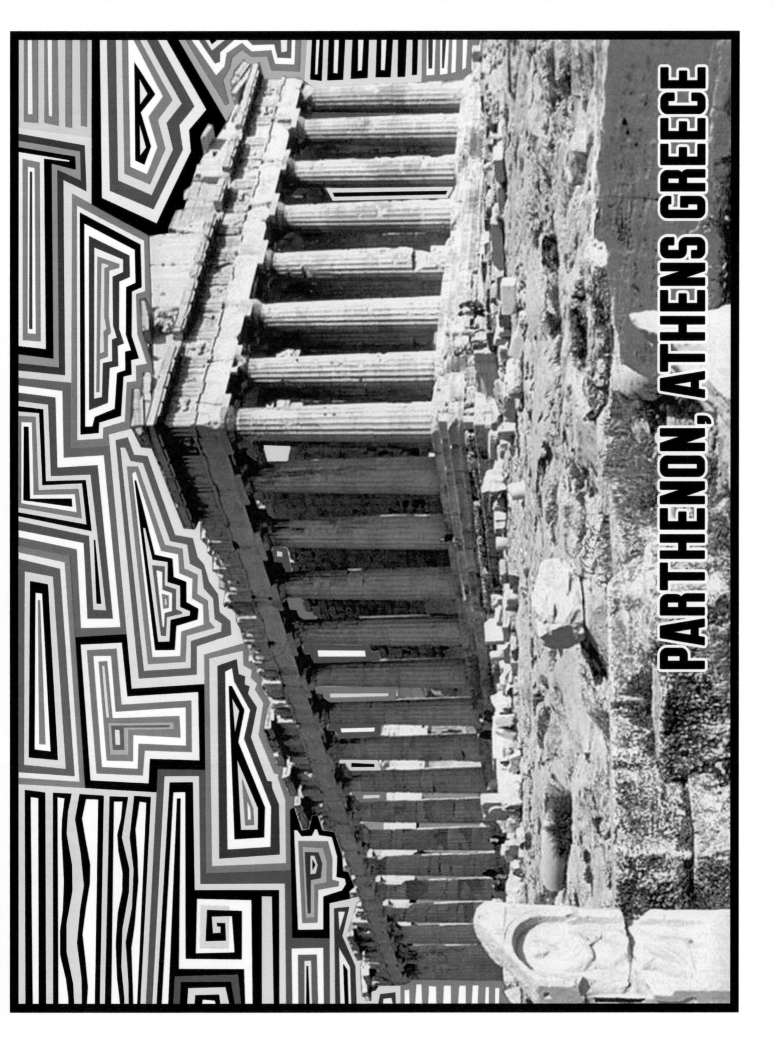

PARTHENON, ATHENS GREECE

AT ITS ECONOMIC HEIGHT, IN THE 5TH AND 4TH CENTURIES BC, ANCIENT GREECE WAS THE MOST ADVANCED ECONOMY IN THE WORLD.

EUCLID WAS A GREEK MATHEMATICIAN WHO IS REFERRED TO AS THE 'FATHER OF GEOMETRY'.

HIPPOCRATES IS OFTEN CALLED "THE FATHER OF WESTERN MEDICINE" BECAUSE HE STARTED ONE OF THE FIRST MEDICAL SCHOOLS IN ANCIENT GREECE.

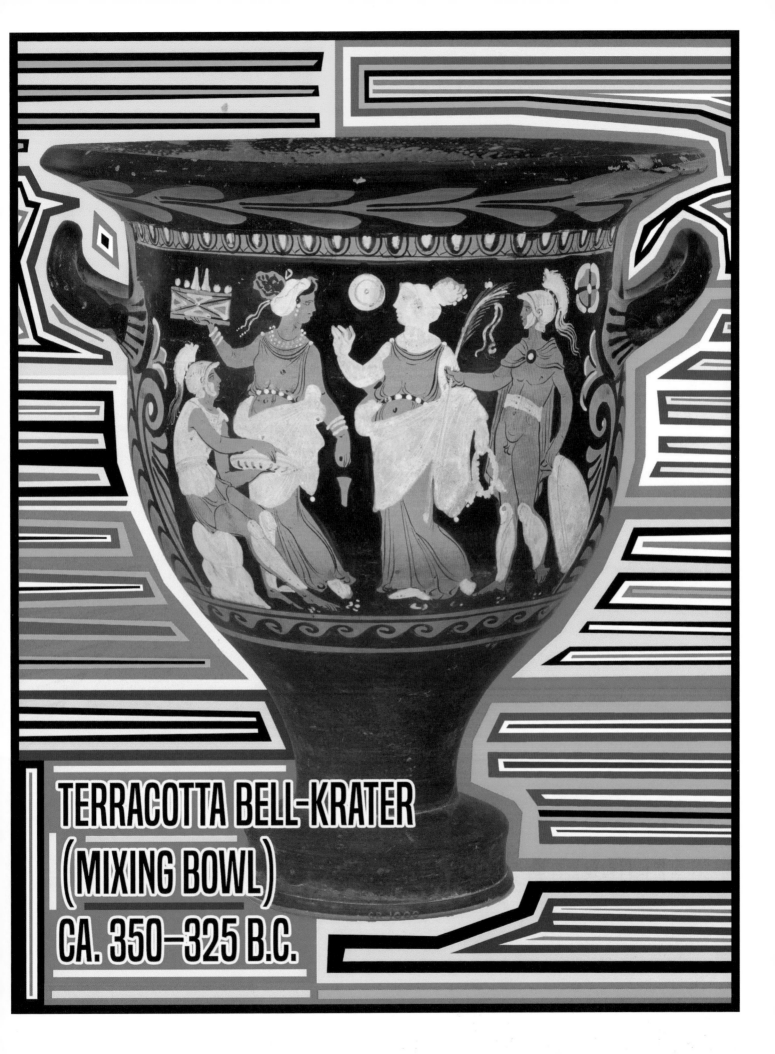

TERRACOTTA BELL-KRATER
(MIXING BOWL)
CA. 350–325 B.C.

IN ANCIENT GREEK, THE WORD "DIOT" MEANT ANYONE WHO WASN'T A POLITICIAN.

GREEK HERO "HERAKLES"

THE ERECHTHEUM
ACROPOLIS
ATHENS, GREECE

SOCRATES WAS ONE OF THE MOST FAMOUS PHILOSOPHERS OF HIS TIME. HE IS ALSO KNOWN AS 'THE FATHER OF WESTERN THOUGHT'. HE WAS BORN IN ATHENS, GREECE AROUND 470 BC.

ANCIENT GREEKS AND ROMANS
OFTEN BOUGHT SLAVES WITH SALT.
THIS IS WHERE THE PHRASE
NOT WORTH HIS SALT COMES FROM.

THE DISCOVERIES OF GREEK MATHEMATICIANS SUCH AS PYTHAGORAS, EUCLID, AND ARCHIMEDES, ARE STILL USED IN MATHEMATICAL TEACHING TODAY.

"QUALITY IS NOT AN ACT, IT IS A HABIT." –ARISTOTLE

TERRACOTTA OINOCHOE (JUG)
MID-4TH CENTURY B.C.

SERAPIS, GRECO-EGYPTIAN DEITY OF THE SUN

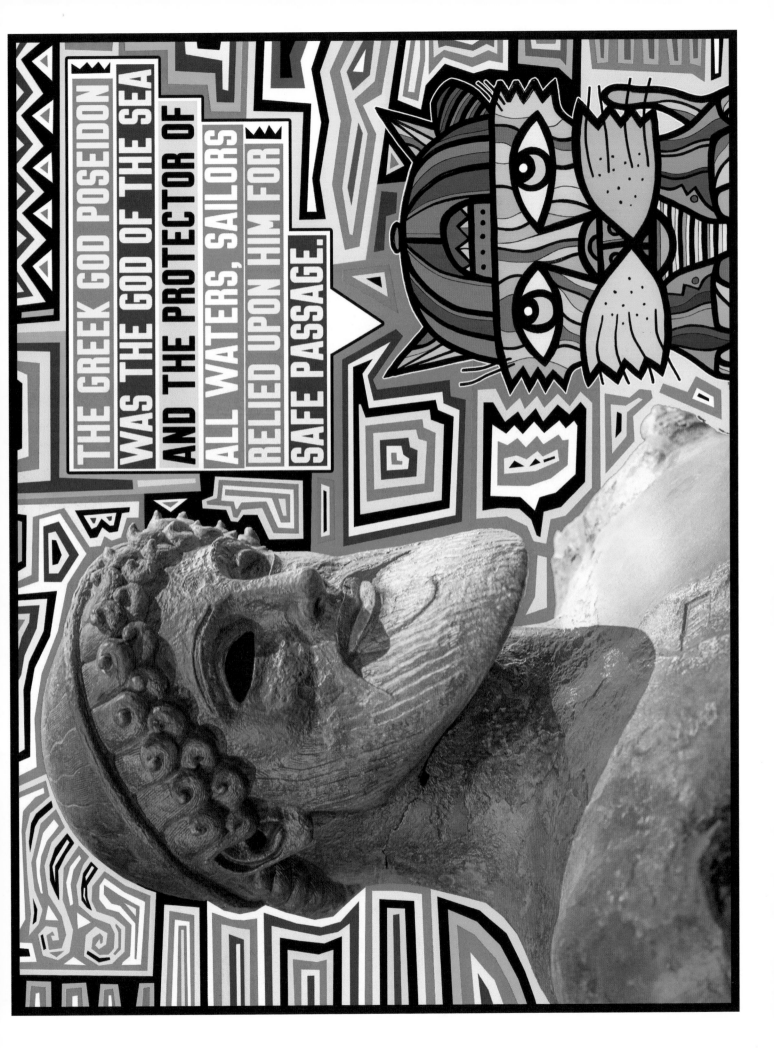

THE TEMPLE OF ATHENA NIKE

PLATO WAS ONE OF THE GREATEST CLASSICAL GREEK PHILOSOPHERS. HE WAS A STUDENT OF SOCRATES AND THE TEACHER OF ARISTOTLE.

THE PARTHENON ONCE BECAME A CHURCH AND A MOSQUE.

PERICLES WAS AN IMPORTANT POPULIST POLITICAL LEADER IN THE DEVELOPMENT OF ATHENIAN DEMOCRACY.

TEMPLE OF HEPHAESTUS
ATHENS, GREECE

"EVERYTHING FLOWS, AND NOTHING ABIDES, EVERYTHING GIVES WAY, AND NOTHING STAYS FIXED."
-HERACLITUS

ANCIENT GREECE USED A CURRENCY KNOWN AS THE DRACHMA. THE DRACHMA WAS ONE OF THE WORLD'S EARLIEST COINS.

TERRACOTTA LEKYTHOS (OIL FLASK)
CA. 550–530 B.C.

DIONYSOS WAS THE GOD OF WINE, VEGETATION, PLEASURE, FESTIVITY, MADNESS AND WILD FRENZY.

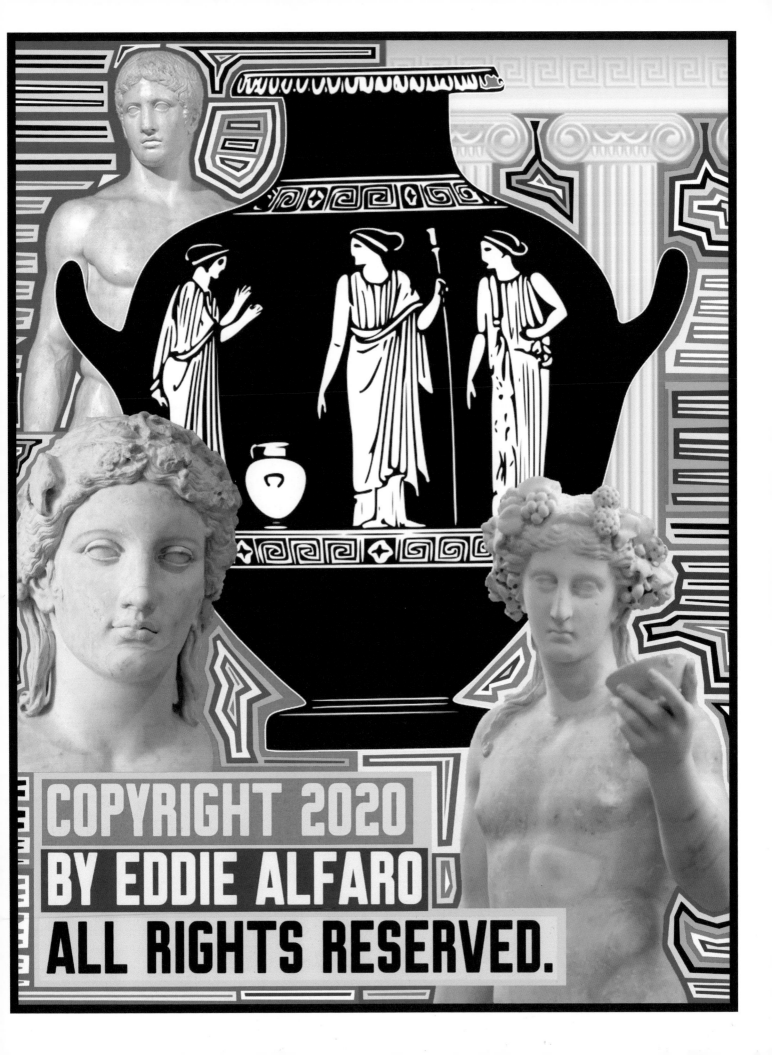

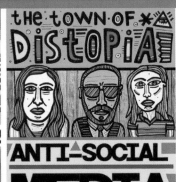
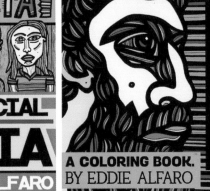
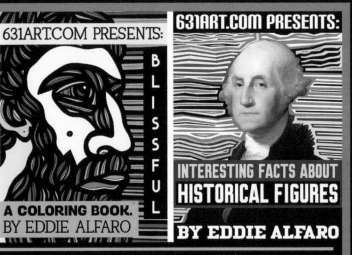

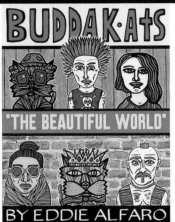

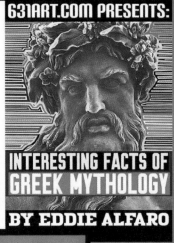

Printed in Great Britain
by Amazon

42178161R00041